Christian Initiation: Additional Baptism Texts in Accessible Language

with Guidance on Using the Alternative Texts

Church House Publishing

Published by | Church House Publishing
Church House
Great Smith Street
London SW1P 3AZ

Copyright © | *The Archbishops' Council 2015*

First published 2015

ISBN | 978-0-7151-2312-6

Printed and bound by Core Publications Limited, Kettering
Typeset in Gill Sans and Joanna by Hugh Hillyard-Parker
Common Worship design by Derek Birdsall RDI and John Morgan

Contents

¶ Authorization

Christian Initiation: Additional Texts for Holy Baptism in Accessible Language have been approved under Canon B 2 of the Canons of the Church of England for use until further resolution of the General Synod.

Canon B 3 provides that in the case of the occasional offices (other than Confirmation), the decision as to which of the authorized forms of service is to be used is to be made by the minister conducting the service, subject to the right of any of the persons concerned to object beforehand to the form of service proposed.

Introduction

The alternative Baptism Texts have been prepared and authorized in response to a motion by the Liverpool Diocesan Synod requesting texts in language that is more accessible to many of those who ask for baptism. It was recognized that the Decision and the Prayer over the Water in the *Common Worship: Christian Initiation* rites were particularly difficult for many. The General Synod accepted this need, and these texts are the result of much careful work.

What we describe as the 'language' of faith includes not only words and actions but also a culture of understanding what the Church, the Bible, the Sacraments and prayer are for. In many parishes this language or culture of faith is not shared by many of those with a deep spiritual yearning and who ask for baptism because they want the very best for their children or for themselves. Clergy and others involved in the ministry of baptism are urged to read the following notes and commentary with care, in addition to the helpful Introduction provided in *Common Worship: Christian Initiation*.

Guidance on Using the
Alternative Baptism Texts

based on notes prepared by the Liturgical Commission

Notes

The new texts, comprising
¶   Presentation of the Candidates,
¶   The Decision,
¶   Signing with the Cross,
¶   Prayer over the Water and
¶   Commission,
are all alternatives to the existing provision in *Common Worship: Christian Initiation*. Any one of the five sections may be substituted for the equivalent section in *Common Worship*. It is not necessary to use all the alternative sections together. However, each of these sections has an integral structure, so where one of the alternative sections is used, that section should be used in its entirety: existing and additional provision should not be combined within a given section.

To make a baptism service accessible to those who are not used to being in church is to think seriously both about the texts that are to be used and about the way the whole rite is articulated – we might say performed. A rite consists of more than words: movement, action, silence and gesture are also of primary importance.

The baptismal liturgy in *Common Worship* is formed on the assumption that it will be celebrated at a principal service, preferably the Eucharist. When *Common Worship Baptism* is used as a free-standing service – such as following a principal service on Sundays – it requires adaptation. For instance, a sensitive priest may insert hymns and songs at appropriate points.

What is provided on pages 12 to 30 is the basic simplified track through the *Common Worship Baptism* liturgy as a separate service, using the alternative forms. The mandatory elements are indicated with a vertical line on the left of the page.

The responses in the alternative material have been simplified, not least to help those who are not confident speaking from a printed text.

When that is the case, a sensitive priest will lead the people to make the responses at the appropriate time.

The Greeting

Frequently parents ask people who have not been baptized to be godparents. This may be a good pastoral opportunity to lead godparents to faith and baptism. However, sometimes a priest is left with the difficult task of explaining that people who are not baptized cannot be godparents because it would be asking something of them that they have not yet taken upon themselves. Using parts of *Common Worship: Thanksgiving for the Gift of a Child* is one possible solution to this difficulty and the relevant text is printed in a box on p. 13.

Introduction

Neither the written *Pastoral Introduction* nor the spoken *Introduction* to the service are mandatory texts: parishes may produce their own written introduction and the minister may lead into the service with a scripted or extempore introduction.

The Collect

In contexts where the language of the Collects might present difficulties ministers are encouraged to make use of the Alternative Collects.

The Sermon

The sermon, as a proclamation of the word of the Lord, is an important part of the liturgy. It may take the form of a commentary accompanying the Scriptures as they are read and a succinct explanation of the liturgical actions as they unfold.

Presentation of the Candidates

The Presentation is divided into two options: for infants and for those who can answer for themselves. In the case of children who may not be confident answering for themselves, the priest should use his/her discretion in deciding which form to use. When, at the same service, there are children in both categories, both options may be used.

The use of Mark 10.14 at the baptism of infants is not used as any kind of justification for infant baptism; it is a means of expressing the welcome of Christ and his Church for children, and for the family present at the baptism.

The Decision

The Decision is formed of two pairs of questions. Between the two pairs of questions is the idea of turning around – conversion – and this may be expressed by some action.

¶ The first pair of questions represents a movement of separation from the old order of sin and death, from the old Adam.

¶ The second pair represents a turning towards newness of life and faith in Christ. This can be well expressed through a physical movement of turning; the movement will depend on the layout of the church.

The first pair of questions might typically be answered facing away from the east, and the second pair after turning to face a symbolic location of new life in the risen Christ, such as the font, holy table or Easter candle. (Ministers should think carefully about where they themselves stand at this point, so that the symbolic turning does not appear as a turning towards the minister.)

Signing with the Cross

The roots of this signing lie in the enrolment of catechumens at the beginning of a period of preparation for baptism, a practice that has been renewed in many parishes. The alternative place for the Signing is immediately after the baptism. When the Signing takes place after the Decision, the minister traces the sign of the cross on the candidate's forehead; s/he may use olive oil (also called the oil of catechumens). Parents, godparents and sponsors may also be invited to sign the candidate (with the oil, if desired). There is rich biblical symbolism associated with anointing: it is an image of cleansing, blessing, consecration to God's purpose, and of preparation for athletic contest which is itself an image of 'running the race' of the Christian life (see 1 Samuel 16.13; Psalms 23.5; 45.7; 133.2). Many parishes use oil that has been blessed by the Bishop, and this is a reminder that each individual baptism is also an act of the whole Church.

Prayer over the Water

Given that water is essential to the performance of a baptism and that the symbolism of water is central to the meaning of the rite, it is worth drawing attention to the water. It can be poured into the font from a jug, visibly and audibly, possibly by a godparent, before the Prayer over the Water.

The opening dialogue, 'Praise God who made heaven and earth ...' continues to be appropriate but may be omitted. Two prayers are provided. The first uses the imagery of Moses leading the people to freedom through the Red Sea and Christ's passing through the deep waters of death, leading to prayer that the candidates may die and rise with him and find true freedom as God's children. The second focuses on Christ's baptism in the Jordan when the Spirit came on him and he was revealed as the Son God loves, leading to prayer that the candidates may be cleansed and filled with the Spirit so that they, too, may know they are loved as God's children.

Prayers over the Water are not entirely specific to the individual being baptized so they refer, in the plural, to 'those who are washed in this water' and 'those who are baptized in it [this water]'. There is no need to alter them when one individual is being baptized.

Profession of Faith

The forms provided are those in *Common Worship: Christian Initiation*.

After the Baptism

No change has been made to the option that, immediately after the baptism, the newly baptized may be wrapped in a white scarf or shawl, symbolic of being clothed with Christ.

Anointing with the oil of chrism may accompany the prayer after baptism, possibly by pouring the oil over the crown of the candidate's head. Alternatively, if the Signing with the Cross takes place after baptism (rather than as a response to the Decision), oil of chrism may be used for it, and the symbolism of the act is of witness to Christ crucified. Chrism is a fragrant oil, evoking the presence and joy of Jesus Christ, and the blessings of the Holy Spirit.

Commission

In place of the forms of Commission provided in *Common Worship* two options are provided as alternatives. It is intended that the minister (or other suitable person) will talk directly and simply in his or her own words to the parents, godparents and congregation, or to the newly baptized in the case of the baptism of those able to answer for themselves, covering the topics listed in the bullet-points. Some ministers may find it helpful to speak from these bullet-points, but it is desirable to avoid giving the impression that a written text is simply being read out. As an example, the address might be something like the following:

Parents and godparents, we are glad to have welcomed you here for the baptism of *N and N*. Today *they* have joined us on our Christian journey. Baptism unites us with Christ and to his whole Church, on earth and in heaven.

Here, we shall do all that we can to ensure that there is a welcoming place for you. We will play our part in helping you guide *these children* along the way of faith.

Bringing up children as Christians has its challenges. *N and N* will need to discover the story of Christ's birth, death and resurrection, the pattern of his loving life, and the teaching that he gave. We pray that *they* will come closer to God as *they* grow in faith, explore the Bible, and make *their* baptismal promises for *themselves* when *they* come to confirmation.

As well as worshipping with the Church, Christians follow Jesus by standing up for truth and justice, and showing compassion to those in need. They are to be faithful and loving. The example that you give by prayer and the life that you lead will affect *N and N* for *their* whole life. Remember to ask for God's help, and pray for *them* often, as we now pray for you.

Or, at the baptism of those able to answer for themselves:

N, we are glad to have welcomed you to *(name of church)* for your baptism. There will always be a place for you here. Your baptism joins you to Christ and to his whole Church, in every part of the world, in the past and in the future, on earth and in heaven.

Even before today, God began his work in you, but it will take the whole of your life to complete that work. There will be moments when the journey ahead is a delight and there will be times when it is hard, but you will never be alone. You will always have the support of other Christians. There will be many milestones on your journey: confirmation will be one of them.

Remember that in Jesus heaven has touched our world. Belonging to him will change your life and, through reading the Bible, you will learn more deeply the story of God's love. Through worship, prayer and caring for others you will grow more and more like Jesus. Stand up for fairness, truth and kindness.

God's love is for you, and for everyone. Share with other people the good news of his love.

Welcoming someone into the congregation

When a baptism is celebrated within Holy Communion, the Welcome and Peace should follow, rather than precede, the Prayers of Intercession.

Since a baptism is a public event, where a baptism has taken place at a separate service, the family may be invited to return at a principal service for the child to be welcomed by the wider congregation.

The Giving of a Candle

Many parishes give a candle to the newly baptized; this may be lit from the Easter candle in churches which use one, and will sometimes be a miniature copy of the Easter candle. It needs to be clearly explained that the candle is for the family to take home. They may be encouraged to light it on birthdays, on the anniversary of baptism or on other special occasions.

Page numbers

See *Common Worship: Christian Initiation*, CHP 2006 ISBN 0 7151 2102 2

Holy Baptism

* Indicates alternative texts

¶ **Preparation**

The Greeting
[Optional Thanksgiving Prayer and Presentation of a Gospel]
Introduction
The Collect [of the day or as printed]

¶ **The Liturgy of the Word**

Reading(s)
Gospel Reading
Sermon [see note]

¶ **The Liturgy of Baptism**

Presentation of the Candidates*
The Decision*
     Signing with the Cross* [alternative position below]
Prayer over the Water* [two alternatives]
Profession of Faith [two alternatives]
Baptism
     [Signing with the Cross may take place at this point]
Commission*
The Welcome and Peace
Prayers of Intercession [two alternatives provided;
     others may be used]
The Lord's Prayer

¶ **The Sending Out**

The Blessing
Giving of a Lighted Candle
The Dismissal

*When these texts are used in conjunction with Holy Communion
or Morning and Evening Prayer, see* Common Worship:
Initiation Services *for details.*

Pastoral Introduction

Baptism marks the beginning of a journey with God which continues for the rest of our lives, the first step in response to God's love. For all involved, particularly the candidates but also parents, godparents and sponsors, it is a joyful moment when we rejoice in what God has done for us in Christ, making serious promises and declaring the faith. The wider community of the local church and friends welcome the new Christian, promising support and prayer for the future. Hearing and doing these things provides an opportunity to remember our own baptism and reflect on the progress made on that journey, which is now to be shared with this new member of the Church.

The service paints many vivid pictures of what happens on the Christian way. There is the sign of the cross, the badge of faith in the Christian journey, which reminds us of Christ's death for us. Our 'drowning' in the water of baptism, where we believe we die to sin and are raised to new life, unites us to Christ's dying and rising, a picture that can be brought home vividly by the way the baptism is administered. Water is also a sign of new life, as we are born again by water and the Spirit. This reminds us of Jesus' baptism. And as a sign of that new life, there may be a lighted candle, a picture of the light of Christ conquering the darkness of evil. Everyone who is baptized walks in that light for the rest of their lives.

As you pray for the candidates, picture them with yourself and the whole Church throughout the ages, journeying into the fullness of God's love.

**Jesus said, 'I came that they may have life,
and have it abundantly.'**
John 10.10

Holy Baptism

A Sample Service using the Additional Texts

¶ Preparation

At the entry of the ministers a hymn may be sung.

The Greeting

The grace of our Lord Jesus Christ,
the love of God
and the fellowship of the Holy Spirit
be with you all

All **and also with you.**

Words of welcome or introduction may be said.
The president may use this prayer of thanksgiving

God our Creator,
we thank you for the wonder of new life
and for the mystery of human love.
We give thanks for all whose support and skill
surround and sustain the beginning of life.
As Jesus knew love and discipline within a human family,
may *these children* grow in strength and wisdom.
As Mary knew the joys and pains of motherhood,
give *these parents* your sustaining grace and love;
through Jesus Christ our Lord.

All **Amen.**

The minister says

Do you receive *these children* as a gift from God?
We do.

Do you wish to give thanks to God and seek his blessing?
We do.

Will you do all that you can to help and support *N and N* in the bringing up of *N*?
With the help of God we will.

A copy of a Gospel is presented, with these words

Receive this book.
It is the good news of God's love.
Take it as your guide.

Introduction

The president introduces the sacrament of baptism,
using these or other words.
(For seasonal Introductions, see pages 150–165.)

Our Lord Jesus Christ has told us
that to enter the kingdom of heaven
we must be born again of water and the Spirit,
and has given us baptism as the sign and seal of this new birth.
Here we are washed by the Holy Spirit and made clean.
Here we are clothed with Christ,
dying to sin that we may live his risen life.
As children of God, we have a new dignity
and God calls us to fullness of life.

The Gloria in excelsis may be used at Holy Communion.
(The candidates may be presented at this point.)

The Collect

The president introduces a period of silent prayer with the words
'Let us pray' or a more specific bidding.
Either the Collect of the Day or this Collect is said. (For seasonal
Collects, see pages 150–165.)

Heavenly Father,
by the power of your Holy Spirit
you give to your faithful people new life in the water
    of baptism.
Guide and strengthen us by the same Spirit,
that we who are born again may serve you in faith and love,
and grow into the full stature of your Son, Jesus Christ,
who is alive and reigns with you in the unity of the Holy Spirit
now and for ever.

All   **Amen.**

¶ The Liturgy of the Word

Readings

The readings of the day are normally used on Sundays, Principal Feasts, other Principal Holy Days and Festivals. (For other occasions, see pages 150–165 and 167.)

Either one or two readings from Scripture may precede the Gospel reading.

At the end the reader may say

This is the word of the Lord.

All **Thanks be to God.**

A psalm or canticle may follow the first reading; other hymns and songs may be used between the readings.

Gospel Reading

An acclamation may herald the Gospel reading.

When the Gospel is announced the reader says

Hear the Gospel of our Lord Jesus Christ according to *N.*

All **Glory to you, O Lord.**

At the end

This is the Gospel of the Lord.

All **Praise to you, O Christ.**

Sermon
(See note)

¶ The Liturgy of Baptism

Presentation of the Candidates

The candidates may be presented to the congregation.
Where appropriate, they may be presented by their
godparents or sponsors.

Either *At the baptism of infants, the president addresses the whole*
congregation

Jesus said, 'Let the children come to me. Do not stop
them'.

We thank God for *N and N* who *have* come to be
baptized today.
Christ loves *them* and welcomes *them* into his Church.

So I ask you all:

Will you support *these children* as *they begin their* journey
of faith?

All **We will.**

Will you help *them* to live and grow within God's family?

All **We will.**

The president then addresses the parents and godparents

God knows each of us by name and we are his.
Parents and godparents, you speak for *N and N* today.
Will you pray for *them*,
and help *them* to follow Christ?
We will.

Or *The president asks those candidates for baptism who are able to answer for themselves*

Do you wish to be baptized?
I do.

Testimony by the candidate(s) may follow.

The president addresses the whole congregation

We thank God for *N and N* who *have* come to be baptized today.
Christ loves *them* and welcomes *them* into his Church.
Will you support *them* on *their* journey of faith?
All   **We will.**

The Decision

The president addresses the candidates directly, or through their parents, godparents and sponsors

We all wander far from God and lose our way:
Christ comes to find us and welcomes us home.
In baptism we respond to his call.

Therefore I ask:

Do you turn away from sin?
I do.

Do you reject evil?
I do.

The candidates, together with their parents, godparents and sponsors, may turn at this point.

Do you turn to Christ as Saviour?
I do.

Do you trust in him as Lord?
I do.

Signing with the Cross

The president or another minister makes the sign of the cross on the forehead of each candidate, saying

Christ claims you for his own.
Receive the sign of his cross.

The president may invite parents, godparents and sponsors to sign the candidates with the cross.

When all the candidates have been signed, the president says

Do not be ashamed of Christ.
You are his for ever.

All   **Stand bravely with him
against all the powers of evil,
and remain faithful to Christ to the end of your life.**

May almighty God deliver you from the powers of darkness,
and lead you in the light and obedience of Christ.

All   **Amen.**

Prayer over the Water

The ministers and candidates gather at the baptismal font.

A canticle, psalm, hymn or litany may be used (see pages 169–176).

(Optional seasonal and responsive forms of the Prayer are provided on pages 150–165 and 177.)

The president stands before the water of baptism and says one of the following prayers

Praise God who made heaven and earth,

All   **who keeps his promise for ever.**

Let us give thanks to the Lord our God.

All   **It is right to give thanks and praise.**

Either

> Loving Father,
> we thank you for your servant Moses,
> who led your people through the waters of the Red Sea
> to freedom in the Promised Land.
> We thank you for your Son Jesus,
> who has passed through the deep waters of death
> and opened for all the way of salvation.
> Now send your Spirit,
> that those who are washed in this water
> may die with Christ and rise with him,
> to find true freedom as your children,
> alive in Christ for ever.

All **Amen.**

Or

> We praise you, loving Father,
> for the gift of your Son Jesus.
> He was baptized in the River Jordan,
> where your Spirit came upon him
> and revealed him as the Son you love.
> He sent his followers
> to baptize all who turn to him.
> Now, Father, we ask you to bless this water,
> that those who are baptized in it
> may be cleansed in the water of life,
> and, filled with your Spirit,
> may know that they are loved as your children,
> safe in Christ for ever.

All **Amen.**

Profession of Faith

One of the following professions of faith is used.

The president addresses the congregation

Either

Let us affirm,
together with *these* who *are* being baptized,
our common faith in Jesus Christ.

Do you believe and trust in God the Father,
source of all being and life,
the one for whom we exist?

All　**I believe and trust in him.**

Do you believe and trust in God the Son,
who took our human nature,
died for us and rose again?

All　**I believe and trust in him.**

Do you believe and trust in God the Holy Spirit,
who gives life to the people of God
and makes Christ known in the world?

All　**I believe and trust in him.**

This is the faith of the Church.

All　**This is our faith.**
We believe and trust in one God,
Father, Son and Holy Spirit.

Or

Brothers and sisters, I ask you to profess
together with *these candidates*
the faith of the Church.

Do you believe and trust in God the Father?

All **I believe in God, the Father almighty,
creator of heaven and earth.**

Do you believe and trust in his Son Jesus Christ?

All **I believe in Jesus Christ, his only Son, our Lord,
who was conceived by the Holy Spirit,
born of the Virgin Mary,
suffered under Pontius Pilate,
was crucified, died, and was buried;
he descended to the dead.
On the third day he rose again;
he ascended into heaven,
he is seated at the right hand of the Father,
and he will come to judge the living and the dead.**

Do you believe and trust in the Holy Spirit?

All **I believe in the Holy Spirit,
the holy catholic Church,
the communion of saints,
the forgiveness of sins,
the resurrection of the body,
and the life everlasting.
Amen.**

Baptism

If the candidate(s) can answer for themselves, the president may say to each one

N, is this your faith?

Each candidate answers in their own words, or says

This is my faith.

The president or another minister dips each candidate in water, or pours water on them, saying

N, I baptize you
in the name of the Father,
and of the Son,
and of the Holy Spirit.

All   **Amen.**

If the newly baptized are clothed with a white robe, a hymn or song may be used, and then a minister may say

You have been clothed with Christ.
As many as are baptized into Christ have put on Christ.

If those who have been baptized were not signed with the cross immediately after the Decision, the president signs each one now.

The president says

May God, who has received you by baptism
    into his Church,
pour upon you the riches of his grace,
that within the company of Christ's pilgrim people
you may daily be renewed by his anointing Spirit,
and come to the inheritance of the saints in glory.

All   **Amen.**

The president and those who have been baptized may return from the font.

Commission

A minister (or another person) addresses the congregation, parents and godparents

Either *Where the newly baptized are unable to answer for themselves, the address includes*

¶ *The welcome of the Church, local and universal*
¶ *The importance of belonging to the Christian community*
¶ *The responsibilities of parents and godparents*
¶ *The challenge to grow in Christian discipleship*

Or *Where the newly baptized are able to answer for themselves, a minister addresses them.*

The address includes

¶ *The welcome of the Church, local and universal*
¶ *The importance of belonging to the Christian community*
¶ *The challenge to grow in Christian discipleship*
¶ *The call to share God's love*

One or more of the following prayers may be used

Faithful and loving God,
bless those who care for *these children*
and grant them your gifts of love, wisdom and faith.
Pour upon them your healing and reconciling love,
and protect their homes from all evil.
Fill them with the light of your presence
and establish them in the joy of your kingdom,
through Jesus Christ our Lord.

All   **Amen.**

God of grace and life,
in your love you have given us
a place among your people;
keep us faithful to our baptism,
and prepare us for that glorious day
when the whole creation will be made perfect
in your Son our Saviour Jesus Christ.

All   **Amen.**

The Welcome and Peace

There is one Lord, one faith, one baptism:
N and N, by one Spirit we are all baptized into one body.

All **We welcome you into the fellowship of faith;**
we are children of the same heavenly Father;
we welcome you.

The congregation may greet the newly baptized.

The president introduces the Peace in these or other seasonal words (see pages 150–165)

We are all one in Christ Jesus.
We belong to him through faith,
heirs of the promise of the Spirit of peace.

The peace of the Lord be always with you

All **and also with you.**

A minister may say

Let us offer one another a sign of peace.

All may exchange a sign of peace.

Prayers of Intercession

Intercessions may be led by the president or others.

Either of the following or other suitable words may be used.
(For seasonal forms, see pages 150–165.)

1.

As a royal priesthood, let us pray to the Father
through Christ who ever lives to intercede for us.

Reveal your kingdom among the nations;
may peace abound and justice flourish.
Especially for …
Your name be hallowed.

All **Your kingdom come.**

Send down upon us the gift of the Spirit
and renew your Church with power from on high.
Especially for …
Your name be hallowed.

All **Your kingdom come.**

Deliver the oppressed, strengthen the weak,
heal and restore your creation.
Especially for …
Your name be hallowed.

All **Your kingdom come.**

Rejoicing in the fellowship of the Church on earth,
we join our prayers with all the saints in glory.
Your name be hallowed.

All **Your kingdom come.**

2.

We thank you that you have claimed for yourself
those who have been washed in the waters of rebirth.
Uphold them in this new life,
that they may ever remain steadfast in faith,
joyful in hope, and rooted in your love.
Father of life,

All **make known your glory.**

Pour your blessing on all your people.
May our hearts ever praise you,
and find their perfect rest in you.
Grant us the freedom of your service
and peace in doing your will.
Father of life,

All **make known your glory.**

The whole creation is filled with the light of your grace.
Dispel the darkness of our hearts, and forgive our sins
and negligences,
that we may come at last to the light of your glory.
Father of life,

All **make known your glory.**

The Lord's Prayer

As your children, born again in Christ, we say

Either

All **Our Father in heaven,**
hallowed be your name,
your kingdom come,
your will be done,
on earth as in heaven.
Give us today our daily bread.
Forgive us our sins
as we forgive those who sin against us.
Lead us not into temptation
but deliver us from evil.
For the kingdom, the power,
and the glory are yours
now and for ever.
Amen.

Or

All **Our Father, who art in heaven,**
hallowed be thy name;
thy kingdom come;
thy will be done;
on earth as it is in heaven.
Give us this day our daily bread.
And forgive us our trespasses,
as we forgive those who trespass against us.
And lead us not into temptation;
but deliver us from evil.
For thine is the kingdom,
the power and the glory,
for ever and ever.
Amen.

¶ The Sending Out

The Blessing

The president may use a seasonal blessing (pages 150–165), or another suitable blessing, or

The God of all grace,
who called you to his eternal glory in Christ Jesus,
establish, strengthen and settle you in the faith;
and the blessing of God almighty,
the Father, the Son, and the Holy Spirit,
be among you and remain with you always.

All **Amen.**

Giving of a Lighted Candle

The minister or another person may give all the newly baptized a lighted candle. These may be lit from the candle used at the Decision.

When all have received a candle, the minister says

God has delivered us from the dominion of darkness
and has given us a place with the saints in light.
You have received the light of Christ;
walk in this light all the days of your life.

All **Shine as a light in the world,
to the glory of God the Father.**

The Dismissal

Go in the light and peace of Christ.

All **Thanks be to God.**

From Easter Day to Pentecost

Go in the light and peace of Christ. Alleluia, alleluia.

All **Thanks be to God. Alleluia, alleluia.**

Christian Initiation: Additional Texts for Holy Baptism in Accessible Language

Presentation of the Candidates

The candidates may be presented to the congregation. Where appropriate, they may be presented by their godparents or sponsors.

Either

At the baptism of infants, the president addresses the whole congregation

Jesus said, 'Let the children come to me. Do not stop them'.

We thank God for *N and N* who *have* come to be baptized today. Christ loves *them* and welcomes *them* into his Church.

So I ask you all:

Will you support *these children* as *they begin their* journey of faith?

All **We will.**

Will you help *them* to live and grow within God's family?

All **We will.**

The president then addresses the parents and godparents

God knows each of us by name and we are his.
Parents and godparents, you speak for *N and N* today.
Will you pray for *them*,
and help *them* to follow Christ?
We will.

Or

The president asks those candidates for baptism who are able to answer for themselves

Do you wish to be baptized?
I do.

Testimony by the candidate(s) may follow.

The president addresses the whole congregation

We thank God for *N and N* who *have* come to be baptized today.
Christ loves *them* and welcomes *them* into his Church.
Will you support *them* on *their* journey of faith?

All **We will.**

The Decision

The president addresses the candidates directly, or through their parents, godparents and sponsors

We all wander far from God and lose our way:
Christ comes to find us and welcomes us home.
In baptism we respond to his call.

Therefore I ask:

Do you turn away from sin?
I do.

Do you reject evil?
I do.

The candidates, together with their parents, godparents and sponsors, may turn at this point.

Do you turn to Christ as Saviour?
I do.

Do you trust in him as Lord?
I do.

Signing with the Cross

The president or another minister makes the sign of the cross on the forehead of each candidate, saying

Christ claims you for his own.
Receive the sign of his cross.

The president may invite parents, godparents and sponsors to sign the candidates with the cross.

When all the candidates have been signed, the president says

Do not be ashamed of Christ.
You are his for ever.

All **Stand bravely with him
against all the powers of evil,
and remain faithful to Christ to the end of your life.**

May almighty God deliver you from the powers of darkness,
and lead you in the light and obedience of Christ.

All **Amen.**

Prayer over the Water

Either

Loving Father,
we thank you for your servant Moses,
who led your people through the waters of the Red Sea
to freedom in the Promised Land.
We thank you for your Son Jesus,
who has passed through the deep waters of death
and opened for all the way of salvation.
Now send your Spirit,
that those who are washed in this water
may die with Christ and rise with him,
to find true freedom as your children,
alive in Christ for ever.

All **Amen.**

Or

We praise you, loving Father,
for the gift of your Son Jesus.
He was baptized in the River Jordan,
where your Spirit came upon him
and revealed him as the Son you love.
He sent his followers
to baptize all who turn to him.
Now, Father, we ask you to bless this water,
that those who are baptized in it
may be cleansed in the water of life,
and, filled with your Spirit,
may know that they are loved as your children,
safe in Christ for ever.

All **Amen.**

Commission

Either   *Where the newly baptized are unable to answer for themselves, a minister addresses the congregation, parents and godparents. The address includes*

¶   *The welcome of the Church, local and universal*
¶   *The importance of belonging to the Christian community*
¶   *The responsibilities of parents and godparents*
¶   *The challenge to grow in Christian discipleship*

Or   *Where the newly baptized are able to answer for themselves, a minister addresses them. The address includes*

¶   *The welcome of the Church, local and universal*
¶   *The importance of belonging to the Christian community*
¶   *The challenge to grow in Christian discipleship*
¶   *The call to share God's love*